I0437371

Africa Quiz Book

Quotes - Inspiration - Little Known Facts

by
Jeanette Ivory-Williamson

Bloomington, IN  Milton Keynes, UK
authorHOUSE

AuthorHouse™
1663 Liberty Drive, Suite 200
Bloomington, IN 47403
www.authorhouse.com
Phone: 1-800-839-8640

AuthorHouse™ UK Ltd.
500 Avebury Boulevard
Central Milton Keynes, MK9 2BE
www.authorhouse.co.uk
Phone: 08001974150

© 2006 Jeanette Ivory-Williamson. All rights reserved.

No part of this book may be reproduced, stored in a retrieval system, or transmitted by any means without the written permission of the author.

First published by AuthorHouse 10/16/2006

ISBN: 1-4259-5468-5 (sc)

Library of Congress Control Number: 2006907587

Printed in the United States of America
Bloomington, Indiana

This book is printed on acid-free paper.

Publishers' cataloging in publication
Williamson, Jeanette.
African Quiz Book
Jeanette Williamson – 1ˢᵗ Ed.

Book design by Jeanette Williamson

Artwork on Cover by Kambel Dieng

Kambel Dieng

The artwork on the cover was done by the world-renowned
West African artist, Kambel Dieng. I met Kambel more
than a decade ago in his studio on Gorée Island, two miles
off the coast of Africa. Kambel has exhibited his work in
France, Spain, Germany, and the United States.

Inside his open-air workshop, Kambel paints.
A canvas is carelessly hung on the wall.
Kambel moves back, advances, and looks.
Over the top of the wall, the others look too.

Kambel, almost all of them know him.
They know they can learn from him. They will understand
the why and the how of the line and the color.

The hand grasps the paintbrush and with that movement,
The line is born, the children comment
The colors crash on the canvas.
The adults argue.

The paintings of Kambel are dense, strong
of a tradition and a knowledge perfectly controlled.
In his open-air workshop, in the hubbub of the words and
laughs, Kambel paints.

Born in Kaolack, Senegal in 1953, Kambel is a
Tie-dyer's grandson
He grew up in the colors.

Later he worked with Bocar Diong, who specialized in the elaboration of colors.

The "Thioub" traditional dye techniques became his main fountain of inspiration.

Translated by Adama Condula

Dedicated to my children
Alpha Wilson and Troy A. Foster

and to

Dr. Annette Ivory Dunzo

Carl, Jocelyn, Jerod, Jeremy Wilson,
Tyeteanna Gerald,
Val Tate, Troy Tate, Israel Wright

Derrick Wood, Darrell Wood
Mariama Wood, Naima, Nyaa Wood

Boubacar Joseph Ndiaye

Adama Condula

Kambel and Marthe Dieng

Fayimba Koroma

The memory of
James and Panthy Ivory

Love you.

Acknowledgments

I am deeply grateful to many for their support on this effort. First, I would like to thank God for the vision and for granting me the patience to complete this project. Next, I would like to thank Doris Webster who had confidence in my ability to write and publish this book before the first page was written. Vickie Daniels, thank you for your brutal honesty. Suzanne Burrell, thank you for all your support and suggestions. Troy Foster, thanks for helping me to remain positive. Troy Tate, thanks for your opinions. Roger Matlock, thanks for your support and encouragement. Thanks to my African friends in Africa and America who have broadened my dimensions, expanded my horizons, and enhanced my life by sharing their culture. I complete my list of thanks by saying thanks to Barbara Guyse for sharing her vast knowledge of history and editing skills. Thanks to Dr. Annette Ivory Dunzo of Howard University for her careful reading of the text, review, and editorial comments.

Table of Contents

Introduction

The Africa Quiz Book includes questions that are interesting as well as educational. The questions have been carefully compiled from material found in the author's own book collection, research materials, and various primary sources. The questions were not selected because of their ease or difficulty; I simply looked around my collection of African history books, novels, art, short story collections, and personal West African research materials, and thought about some of the things about those books, documents, and writers that interest and intrigue me.

There are two questions on each page, and the answers, along with sources of information; additional explanatory notes are printed on the back of each page. The first chapter presents questions about the geographic features and the outstanding natural and cultural sites that exist on the continent of Africa. The questions and annotations in Chapter 2 were selected with the information attained from members of a few minority and majority groups of Africa. Places as diverse and unique as the pyramids of and the rock-hewn churches of Ethiopia, examples of Africa's natural and cultural places inscribed on the World Heritage List, are featured in Chapter 3. Several of Africa's Nobel Laureates and their works provide the source materials for questions in Chapter 4. Chapter 5 provides information about Gorée Island and the slave trade as told by Joseph Boubacar Ndiaye, curator of the "Maison des Eslaves" (House of Slaves), located on Gorée Island. Questions and quotations used in Chapter 6 and Chapter 7 are randomly selected from government statistics and primary sources of information.

Typical quiz questions and answers are:

QUESTION

Which country has the largest population in Africa?

 a) Algeria
b) Nigeria
c) Zaire

ANSWER

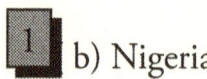

Nigeria has an estimated population of 131.9 million people.
Source: CIA The World Factbook (2006 est.)

QUESTION

Which World Heritage site is located two miles off the coast of Dakar, Senegal?

 a) Gorée Island
b) James Island
c) Robben Island

ANSWER

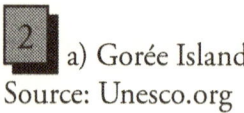
Source: Unesco.org

The *Africa Quiz Book* is meant for a diverse readership. The book contains questions not only about factual information, but some of the areas questioned can help learners explore deeper levels of knowing, thinking, and understanding of African people. The book contains fun facts as well as little-known facts about the world's second largest continent.

Chapter 1: Africa's Geography

This chapter presents questions about the physical, cultural and economic geography of Africa.

 Which continent is the world's second-largest in both area and population?

a) Africa

b) North America

c) Asia

 Which river flows from south to north and is the longest in the Africa?

a) Nile

b) Congo

c) Gambia

ANSWERS

1. (a) Africa

Continents by size: #1 Asia; #2 Africa; #3 North America; #4 South America; #5 Antarctica; #6 Europe; #7 Australia. Africa has 53 countries and a population of more than 850 million people.

Source: *WorldAtlas.com* (2006 est.)

2. (a) Nile

The Nile is approximately 4,160 miles long, but lost a few miles after the completion of the Aswan High Dam near the town of Aswan, Egypt in 1971. The Nile has its origins in Burundi and flows from the mountains in the south to the Mediterranean Sea in the north.

Source: *WorldAtlas.com*

The largest surviving pyramid in the world was built for which of the following pharaohs?

a) Khufu

b) Kafre

c) Menkaure

Which mountain is the highest in Africa?

a) Mount Kilimanjaro

b) Mount Kenya

c) Mount Mawenzi

ANSWERS

3. (a) Khufu

The Great Pyramid at Giza, Egypt was commissioned by Khufu (Cheops) in 2550 BC and had an original estimated height of 481 feet. It is estimated to contain approximately 2.3 million limestone blocks, which weigh about three tons each.

Source: *nationalgeographic.com*

4. (a) Mount Kilimanjaro

Mount Kilimanjaro (19,341 feet), the highest mountain in Africa, is located in northeastern Tanzania, near the Kenyan border.

Source: *Worldatlas.com*

 The largest gold resources in the world were found in which African country?

a) Tanzania

b) South Africa

c) Ghana

 Which country is the world's leading cocoa bean producer?

a) Ethiopia

b) Cote d'Ivoire (Ivory Coast)

c) Ghana

ANSWERS

5. (b) South Africa

South Africa is the world's leading gold producer, and is responsible for approximately one third of the world's annual gold production.

Source: The Gold Institute (2006)

6. (b) Cote d'Ivoire

Cote d'Ivoire is the world's leading producer of cocoa beans, the beans used to produce chocolate. One-third of the world's cocoa comes from Cote d'Ivoire.

Source: International Cocoa Organization (2006)

 Which country is Africa's largest in area?

a) Sudan

b) Ethiopia

c) South Africa

 How many African countries are landlocked?

a) 5

b) 10

c) 15

ANSWERS

7. (a) Sudan

Sudan, the largest country by area in Africa, is the homeland of the Nubian Empire. The inhabitants of southern Egypt and Sudan still refer to themselves as Nubians.

Source: Library of Congress *Countries Studies*

8. (c) 15

Landlocked countries have no access to oceans or seas. The African landlocked countries are Botswana, Burkina Faso, Burundi, Central African Republic, Chad, Ethiopia, Lesotho, Malawi, Mali, Niger, Rwanda, Swaziland, Uganda, Zambia, and Zimbabwe.

Source: CIA *The World Factbook*

 What is the name of Africa's newest country?

a) Eritrea

b) Tanzania

c) Burkina Faso

 Which ocean meets the Atlantic at the southern-most tip of Africa?

a) Pacific

b) Indian

c) Arctic

ANSWERS

9. (a) Eritrea

Eritrea achieved independence on May 24, 1993 from Ethiopia.

Source: U.S. Department of State

10. (b) Indian

Oceans by size: #1 Pacific; #2 Atlantic; #3 Indian; #4 Southern; #5 Arctic.

Source: *WorldAtlas.com*

 Which country has the largest population in Africa?

a) Niger

b) Nigeria

c) Mauritania

 Which country has the second largest population in Africa?

a) Tunisia

b) Egypt

c) Libya

ANSWERS

11. (b) Nigeria

Nigeria has an estimated population of 131.9 million people.
Nigeria, Africa's most populous country, is composed of more than 250 ethnic groups; the following are the most populous and influential: Hausa and Fulani 29%, Yoruba 21%, Igbo (Ibo) 18%, Ijaw 10%, Kanuri 4%, Ibibio 3.5%, Tiv 2.5%

Source: CIA *The World Factbook* (2006 est.)

12. (b) Egypt

Egypt has an estimated population of 70.5 million people. Egypt, Africa's second most populous country, is composed of the following ethnic groups: Eastern Hamitic stock (Egyptians, Bedouins, and Berbers) 99%, Greek, Nubian, Armenian, other European (primarily Italian and French) 1%.

Source: CIA *The World Factbook* (2006 est.)

 Which country is located at the northernmost tip of Africa?

a) Tunisia

b) Morocco

c) Algeria

 Which country is located at the southernmost tip of Africa?

a) Swaziland

b) South Africa

c) Lesotho

ANSWERS

13. (a) Tunisia

Tunisia, located on the northern tip of Africa just across the Mediterranean from the Italian island of Sicily, is between Algeria and Libya.

Source: CIA *The World Factbook*

14. (b) South Africa

South Africa, located on the southern tip of Africa, borders the countries of Namibia, Botswana, Zimbabwe, Mozambique, and Swaziland.

Source: CIA *The World Factbook*

Chapter 2: African Ethnic Groups

There are many different ethnic groups across the continent of Africa. Each ethnic group has its own distinct language, traditions, arts and crafts, history, way of life, and religion.

This chapter presents questions about some of the more widely known ethnic groups in Africa.

 Which ethnic group inhabits the Kalahari Desert?

a) San/Bushmen

b) Akan

c) Ewe

 Zulu is a the name of an ethnic group in which African country?

a) South Africa

b) Senegal

c) Ghana

ANSWERS

15. (a) San/Bushmen

The San/Bushmen people of the Kalahari occupied South Africa as early as 20,000 years ago.

Source: The Library of Congress *Country Studies*

16. (a) South Africa

In the 1990s, it was estimated that 8 million South Africans considered themselves Zulu.

Source: The Library of Congress *Country Studies*

 Which ethnic group lives in southwest Nigeria and Benin?

a) Wolof

b) Yoruba

c) Fulani

 Which ethnic group, famous as herders and warriors once dominated the plains of East Africa?

a) Maasai

b) Ewe

c) Wolof

ANSWERS

17. (b) Yoruba

The Osun Sacred Grove, a symbol of identity for all Yoruba people was inscribed on UNESCO's World Heritage List in 2005.

Source: *Unesco.org*

18. (a) Maasai

The traditional Maasai diet consisted of meat, milk, and blood from cattle. Traditional beliefs were that the use of land to raise crops was a crime against nature.

Source: *maasai-association.org*

 Which West African ethnic group built their houses in the shelter of the pink sandstone cliffs of Bandiagara in Mali?

a) Dogon

b) Mandinka

c) Akan

 The majority of Senegalese people belong to which ethnic group?

a) Mandinka

b) Creole

c) Wolof

ANSWERS

19. (a) Dogon

The Dogon built their houses below the Bandiagara cliffs to prevent attacks by warriors.

Source: Vanbeek, E. A. *Dogon: Africa's People of the Cliff.*_(New York: Harry N. Adams, 2004)

20. (c) Wolof

The Wolof ethnic group makes up 43.3% of Senegal's population. Wolof is the native language of the Wolof people.

Source: CIA *The World Factbook* (2006 est.)

 The Ashanti (also known as the Asante) live in which West African country?

a) Morocco

b) Ghana

c) Niger

 Which African ethnic group is the tallest in the world?

a) Tutsi (aka) Watussi

b) Massai

c) Ebo

ANSWERS

21. (b) Ghana

The Ashanti's king is known as the Asantehene.

Source: Library of Congress *Country Studies*

22. (a) Tutsi

The tallest major ethnic group in the world is the Tutsi (also known as the Watussi) tribe of Rwanda and Burundi, whose young adult males average six feet. Many of the adult males are more than seven feet tall.

Source: Guinness World Records

 In which region of Africa do the majority of Berbers live?

a) North Africa

b) West Africa

c) Southern Africa

 Which African ethnic group lives along the coastline of East Africa from Somalia to Mozambique?

a) Swahili (Waswahili)

b) Berber

c) Fulani

ANSWERS

23. (a) North Africa

For many centuries, the Berbers inhabited the coast of North Africa from Egypt to the Atlantic Ocean. The Berbers are found as far south as northern Nigeria and as far north as Morocco.

Source: *bbc.co.uk*

24. (a) Swahili

"Kiswahili" is the Swahili word for the Swahili language and "Waswahili" is the Swahili name for the people.

Source: *www.wikipedia.com*

 Who are the historians, storytellers, traditional praise singers , and musicians that pass down the oral history of West Africans?

a) Griots

b) storytellers

c) historians

 Which ethnic group were once nomads throughout the Sahara Desert?

a) Wolof

b) Tuareg

c) Zulu

ANSWERS

25. (a) Griots

"A *Griot* is an oral historian and musician," explains Foday Musa Suso, one of West Africa's most respected and well-known contemporary *Griots*. "*Griots* were trusted court advisors to the kings of West Africa from the twelfth century to the twentieth century."

26. (b) Tuareg

The Tuareg of the Sahara Desert are often referred to as "Blue Men of the desert." The Tuareg men are known for the practice of veiling their faces with a blue, indigo-dyed cloth.

Source: *www.wikipedia.com*

Chapter 3: Africa's World Heritage Sites

Countries that have pledged to protect their natural and cultural heritage can submit nomination proposals for properties on their territory to be considered for inclusion in UNESCO's (United Nations Educational, Scientific and Cultural Organization) World Heritage List.

This chapter presents questions regarding African sites inscribed on UNESCO's World Heritage list.

 World Heritage is the designation given to places throughout the world that have an outstanding value to humanity. These sites are protected and preserved for future generations.

a) True

b) False

 In 1974, skeletal remains found in the "Lower Valley of the Awash" dated back 4 million years. Where is the Lower Valley of the Awash located?

a) Egypt

b) Ethiopia

c) Libya

ANSWERS

27. (a) True

At the end of 2005 there were 812 sites inscribed on the UNESCO's World Heritage List. Each year the World Heritage Committee considers new sites for inscription on the World Heritage List during its annual meeting.

Source: UNESCO's World Heritage List

28. (b) Ethiopia

In 1974, skeletal remains found in Ethiopia's Awash valley, the oldest of which date back at least 4 million years, enabled the famous Lucy to be reconstructed. The Awash Valley was inscribed on UNESCO's World Heritage List in 1980.

Source: UNESCO's World Heritage List

 Which two African countries have sites inscribed on UNESCO's World Heritage List since the list was first established in 1978?

a) Senegal and Ethiopia

b) Egypt and South Africa

c) Ghana and Tanzania

 Which island, inscribed on UNESCO's World Heritage List in 1968, is located two miles off the coast of Senegal?

a) Robben Island

b) Gorée Island

c) James Island

ANSWERS

29. (a) Senegal and Ethiopia

Senegal has seven sites and Ethiopia has four sites inscribed on the UNESCO's World Heritage List.

Source: UNESCO's World Heritage List (2006)

30. (b) Gorée Island

Gorée Island is the historic site off the West African coast where millions of captured men, women, and children were rounded up in chains and sold into slavery.

Source: UNESCO's World Heritage List

 The most famous building on Gorée Island, Senegal is the "Maison des Eslaves" (House of Slaves). Who was the first curator of this slave house?

a) James Smith

b) Boubacar Joseph Ndiaye

c) Cheifo Diop

 Which pope visited the "Maison des Eslaves" (House of Slaves) on Gorée Island in 1992?

a) Pope James

b) Pope John Paul II

c) Pope John XXIII

ANSWERS

31. (b) Boubacar Joseph Ndiaye

Mr. Ndiaye is the curator of the "Maison des Eslaves" (House of Slaves) on Gorée Island.

Source: Ndiaye, Joseph Boubacar. *The Slave House of Gorée Island.* (Senegal: 1995)

32. (b) Pope John Paul II

During Pope John Paul II's visit to the "Maison des Eslaves" (House of Slaves), the pope prayed for forgiveness for the Catholic Church's involvement in the transatlantic slave trade.

Source: *Vatican.va*

In which year was James Island inscribed on UNESCO's World Heritage List?

a) 1963

b) 1965

c) 2003

Which African-American best-selling author traced his roots to Gambia?

a) Alex Haley

b) Cornel West

c) Joel Walker

ANSWERS

33. (c) 2003

Slave stations were built on James Island during the years of the transatlantic slave trade. James Island is located off the coast of Gambia.

Source: UNESCO's World Heritage List

34. (a) Alex Haley (1921-1992)

Alex Haley wrote about his Gambian ancestry in his Pulitzer Prize-winning book, *Roots*.

Source: The Kunta Kinte-Alex Haley Foundation

 Simien National Park, with its uneven mountain peaks and deep valleys, was one of the first sites to be made a World Heritage site by UNESCO. In which year was this Ethiopian site inscribed on the World Heritage List?

a) 1968

b) 1978

c) 2005

 Several thirteenth-century cave churches are located in a mountainous region of Ethiopia. In which year were these eleven cave churches are inscribed on UNESCO's World Heritage List?

a) 1968

b) 1978

c) 2005

ANSWERS

35. (b) 1978

Simien National Park is home to several rare animals such as the Gelada baboon, Simien fox, and the Walia ibex, a goat found nowhere else in the world.

Source: UNESCO's World Heritage List

36. (b) 1978

Each Ethiopian rock-hewn church was carved out of a single block of rock, with its roof at ground level.

Source: UNESCO's World Heritage List

 The Asante Traditional Buildings, inscribed on UNESCO's World Heritage List in 1980, are located in which African country?

a) Mali

b) Ghana

c) Kenya

 The Cliff of Bandiagara, inscribed on UNESCO's World Heritage List in 1989, is located in which African country?

a) Ghana

b) Mali

c) Kenya

ANSWERS

37. (b) Ghana (northeast of Kumasi)

The Asante Buildings are dwellings remaining from the great Asante civilization. They are made of earth, wood, and straw.

Source: UNESCO's World Heritage List

38. (b) Mali

The Bandiagara site is also known as the Land of the Dogons. Some Dogon people still practice their traditions in this region.

Source: UNESCO's World Heritage List

 Victoria Falls, inscribed on UNESCO's World Heritage List in 1989, located at the border between Zambia and Zimbabwe creates a mist that can be seen more than twelve miles away.

a) True

b) False

 What is the name of the most famous political prisoner kept in a maximum-security prison on Robben Island?

a) Nelson Mandela

b) Desmond Tutu

c) Thabo Mbeki

ANSWERS

39. (a) True

The falls are part of two national parks, Mosi-oa-Tunya National Park in Zambia and Victoria Falls National Park in Zimbabwe.

Source: UNESCO's World Heritage List

40. (a) Nelson Mandela

In 1999, Robben Island was inscribed on UNESCO's World Heritage List. Nelson Mandela was kept in prison on Robben Island from 1964 to 1982, before being transferred to Pollsmoor Prison, on the mainland of South Africa. Mandela spent twenty seven years in prison.

Source: Nobel Foundation

Chapter 4: Africa's Nobel Prize Winners

The Nobel Prize is an international award given yearly since 1901 for achievements in physics, chemistry, medicine, literature, and also for peace. In 1968, the Bank of Sweden instituted the prize in economic sciences in memory of Alfred Nobel, founder of the Nobel Prize. In 1901, the first Nobel prizes were awarded on the fifth anniversary of Alfred Nobel's death under the provisions described in his will.

This chapter presents questions regarding Africa's Nobel Prize winners.

 Who was the Nigerian awarded the Nobel Prize for Literature in 1986?

a) Wole Soyinka

b) Toni Morrison

c) Martin Luther King, Jr.

 Who was the South African awarded the Nobel Prize for Peace in 1960?

a) Albert John Lutuli

b) Nelson Mandela

c) Haile Selassie

ANSWERS

41. (a) Wole Soyinka

One of Soyinka's great works, *Myth Literature and the African World,* is a collection of essays, poems, and plays.

Source: The Nobel Foundation

42. (a) Albert John Lutuli

Albert John Lutuli (1898-1967) led 10 million black Africans in their nonviolent campaign for civil rights in South Africa.

Source: The Nobel Foundation

 Bishop Desmond Tutu was born in 1931 in Klerks-dorp, Transvaal. Desmond Tutu was awarded the Nobel Peace Prize in 1984 for his participation in the campaign to end apartheid in South Africa. What is the definition of *apartheid*?

a) Slavery

b) The official policy of racial segregation formerly practiced in the Republic of South Africa.

c) Integration

Nelson Mandela and Frederik Willem de Klerk shared the Nobel Peace Prize for 1993. They were awarded for their work to terminate the apartheid regime, and for laying the foundation for a new democratic South Africa.

a) True

b) False

ANSWERS

43. (b) The official policy of racial segregation established by the South African government in 1948.

The party began a policy of racial segregation known as apartheid, which means "apartness."

Source: The Nobel Foundation

44. (a) True

Frederik Willem de Klerk was born in Johannesburg, South Africa on March 18, 1936. Willem de Klerk lifted the ban on the African National Congress, and released Nelson Mandela from prison.

Nelson Rolihlahla Mandela was born in Transkei, South Africa on July 18, 1918. The South Africans elected Nelson Mandela as president of South Africa on May 9, 1994.

Source: The Nobel Foundation

 The United Nations and Kofi Annan were jointly awarded the Nobel Peace Prize for 2001. Where was Kofi Annan born?

a) New York

b) Ghana

c) South Africa

 Wangari Maathai recognized for her contribution to sustainable development, democracy and peace was awarded Nobel Peace Prize for 2004. Where was Wangari Maathai born?

a) Kenya

b) Angola

c) Ethiopia

ANSWERS

45. (b) Ghana

Kofi Annan was born in Kumasi, Ghana, on April 8, 1938. Annan established a Global HIV/AIDS and Health Fund in 2001.

Source: The Nobel Foundation

46. (a) Kenya

Wangari Maathai was born in Nyeru, Kenya, on April 1, 1940. She was the first woman in East and Central Africa to earn a doctoral degree. Maathai is recognized for her struggle for democracy, human rights, and environmental conservation.

Source: The Nobel Foundation

Muhammad Anwar Al-Sadat (1918-1981), president of Egypt from 1970 until his assassination in 1981, was awarded the Nobel Prize for Peace in 1978.

a) True

b) False

In 1991, Nadine Gordimer was awarded the Nobel Prize. Which one?

a) Literature

b) Peace

c) Medicine

ANSWERS

47. (a) True

Sadat initiated peace negotiations with Israel, an achievement for which he shared the Nobel Peace Prize for 1978 with Israeli prime minister Menachem Begin. Under their leadership, Egypt and Israel made peace with each other in 1979.

Source: The Nobel Foundation

48. (a) Literature

Gordimer was born in Springs, South Africa on Nov. 11, 1923. Gordimer wrote several novels denouncing apartheid. Some of Gordimer's novels were banned in South Africa during the apartheid regime.

Source: The Nobel Foundation

J.M. Coetzee, born in South Africa, was awarded the Nobel Prize in 2003. Which one?

a) Medicine

b) Literature

c) Physics

Which Egyptian novelist was awarded the Nobel Prize in Literature for 1988?

a) Naguib Mahfouz

b) Achebe Chinua

c) Max Theiler

ANSWERS

49. (b) Literature

John Coetzee was born in Cape Town, South Africa, on February 9, 1940. Coetzee was assistant professor of English at State University of New York in Buffalo from 1968-1971. Coetzee was denied permanent residence in the United States.

Source: The Nobel Foundation

50. (a) Naguib Mahfouz

Naguib Mahfouz was born in Cairo, Egypt, on December 11, 1911. Mahfouz began writing when he was seventeen and won acclaim for his short stories depicting urban life.

Source: The Nobel Foundation

Chapter 5: West Africa Before The Europeans

Civilizations were thriving along the coast of West Africa centuries before the arrival of the Portuguese explorers.

This chapter presents questions regarding West Africa before the Europeans.

 The wealthy African empires thriving between 500 and 1600 AD were Ghana, Mali, and Songhai were located in which region of Africa?

a) North

b) West

c) East

 Which African empire traded with Arabs at ports on the Mediterranean coast and with other kingdoms of East Africa on the Red Sea until its fall in the thirteenth century?

a) Zulu

b) Nubia

c) Ghana

ANSWERS

51. (b) West

The Ghana, Mali and Songhai empires had ambitious rulers, great military powers, and complex political and social systems. The wealth of these empires came mainly from their sources of salt and gold.

Source: Library of Congress *Country Studies*

52. (c) Ghana

After the fall of the empire of Ghana in the thirteenth century, the kingdom of Mali rose to greatness under the leadership of King Sundiata.

Source: Library of Congress *Country Studies*

 Which emperor of Mali came to power in 1312?

a) King Tut

b) Mansa Musa

c) King Ali

 During fourteenth century, which great city in Mali became a center of wealth, learning, and culture?

a) Timbuktu

b) Bamako

c) Skiasso

ANSWERS

53. (b) Mansa Musa

Mansa Musa was a devout Muslim and many mosques, universities, schools, and libraries were built under his rule. In 1324, Mansa Musa gave away more than two tons of gold during his pilgrimage to Mecca.

Source: *www.wikipedia.com*

54. (a) Timbuktu

From the early part of the fourteenth century to the late sixteenth century, the city of Timbuktu was an important intellectual and spiritual center of the Islamic world. .

Source: Library of Congress *Ancient Manuscripts*

Which West African kingdom emerged after the fall of the empire of Mali?

a) Songhai

b) Benin

c) Kongo

Great Songhai kings, such as Sunni Ali Ber and Askia Mohammed Toure, extended the Songhai Kingdom farther than Ghana or Mali. Under Askia the Great, Timbuktu attained its height as a center of trade and Muslim scholarship.

a) True

b) False

ANSWERS

55. (a) Songhai

After the fall of the Mali Empire, the Songhai Empire became the largest and most powerful empire in West Africa under the leadership of the Songhai kings.

Source: *pbs.org*

56. (a) True

The Songhai Kingdom went into decline after the death of Askia Mohammed Toure in 1538.

Source: *pbs.org*

In 1591, the Songhai Empire and Timbuktu were invaded by which armies?

a) Moroccan

b) Dutch

c) Portuguese

Why did it take European explorers until the nineteenth century to reach Timbuktu?

a) They were not interested in the city before this time.

b) They did not have maps.

c) They had difficulties surviving the journey across the Sahara Desert.

ANSWERS

57. (a) Moroccan

In 1591, Timbuktu became part of the Moroccan Empire.

Source: *pbs.org*

58. (c) They had difficulties surviving the journey across the Sahara Desert.

Source: *pbs.org*

 Timbuktu's major university was housed in which mosque?

a) Sankore Mosque

b) Moussa Mosque

c) Saheli Mosque

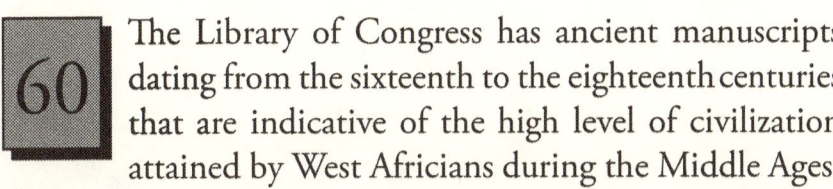 The Library of Congress has ancient manuscripts dating from the sixteenth to the eighteenth centuries that are indicative of the high level of civilization attained by West Africans during the Middle Ages. These manuscripts were taken from the libraries of which African country?

a) Mali

b) Ghana

c) Senegal

ANSWERS

59. (a) Sankore Mosque

The Sankore Mosque is often referred to as the "University of Sankore."

Source: Library of Congress *Ancient Manuscripts*

60. (a) Mali

The Library of Congress has original manuscripts from the libraries of Timbuktu, Mali.

Source: Library of Congress *Ancient Manuscripts*

Chapter 6: The Slave Trade on Gorée Island

More than 20,000 people travel to Gorée Island off the coast of Dakar, Senegal each year to visit the pink stucco Slave House and hear details of how more than 20 million Africans were chained and kept for export. Boubacar Joseph Ndiaye was appointed curator of the *Maison des Enclaves* (House of Slaves) on Gorée Island in 1962 by Leopold Sedar Senghor, Senegal's first president.

This chapter presents questions regarding the slave trade on Gorée Island and its history.

 Which West African country is the westernmost point in Africa.?

a) Gambia

b) Senegal

c) Liberia

 Gorée Island is located two miles off the coast of which West African country?

a) Gambia

b) Senegal

c) Sierra Leone

ANSWERS

61. (b) Senegal

Senegal is the westernmost point in Africa and the closest point to the United States.

Source: Worldatlas.com

62. (a) Senegal

The Island of Gorée is located two miles off the coast of the Dakar, Senegal.

Source: UNESCO's World Heritage List

 Before the arrival of the Europeans, Gorée Island was called BER by its inhabitants.

a) True

b) False

 When did the first Europeans arrive on Gorée Island?

a) 1442

b) 1444

c) 1552

ANSWERS

63. (a) True

Ber was the name given to the Gorée Island before the arrival of the Europeans.

Source: Ndiaye, Joseph Boubacar. *The Slave House of Gorée Island.* (Senegal: 1995)

64. (b) 1444

In 1444, the Portuguese were the first Europeans to set foot on the Gorée Island.

Source: Ndiaye, Joseph Boubacar. *The Slave House of Gorée Island.* (Senegal: 1995)

Every building on Gorée Island was used as slave stations.

a) True

b) False

When was House of Slaves (French: *Maison des esclaves*) built on Gorée Island?

a) 1500

b) 1612

c) 1776

ANSWERS

65. (a) True

Ndiaye states, "Captured Africans were kept in all of the houses on Gorée Island."

Ndiaye, Joseph Boubacar. personal. 20. Feb. 2000.

66. (c) 1776

The House of Slaves (French: *Maison des esclaves*) was built by the Dutch in 1776.

Ndiaye, Joseph Boubacar. personal. 20. Feb. 2000.

Boubacar Joseph Ndiaye was the first principal curator of the House of Slaves (French: *Maison des esclaves*) on Gorée Island.

a) True

b) False

A passageway in the House of Slaves (French: *Maison des esclaves*) leads to the infamous "Door of No Return."

a) True

b) False

ANSWERS

67. (a) True

Ndiaye, Joseph Boubacar. personal. 20. Feb. 2000.

68. (a) True

The Africans who passed through the doorway never came back to their homeland.

Ndiaye, Joseph Boubacar. personal. 20. Feb. 2000.

Chapter 7: Random Facts

This chapter presents questions regarding random African facts.

 The term *diaspora* means the dispersion of a people from their original homeland.

a) True

b) False

 Most African traditional religions produced written works.

a) True

b) False

ANSWERS

69. (a) True

Source: *The American Heritage® Dictionary of the English Language*

70. (b) False

African traditional religions did not produce written works, but were a combination of oral history, custom, and practice, and the power of those gifted in dealing with spiritual issues.

Source: *bbc.co.uk*

 Christianity came first to the continent of Africa in the first or early second century AD.

a) True

b) False

 People of African descent, or specifically the Moors, were in western Europe from AD 710 until the late 1400s.

a) True

b) False

ANSWERS

71. (a) True

The Christian communities in North Africa were among the earliest in the world. Legend states that Christianity was brought from Jerusalem to Alexandria on the Egyptian coast by Mark, one of the four evangelists, in AD 60.

Source: *bbc.co.uk*

72. (a) True

The Moors crossed from Africa into Spain at the beginning of the eighth century.

Source: *www. wikipedia.com*

 The three African Popes of the Roman Catholic Church were from which region of Africa?

a) North

b) South

c) West

 Which African country was not colonized by the Europeans?

a) Ethiopia

b) Liberia

c) Sierra Leone

ANSWERS

73. (a) North

The three African Popes from North Africa are: Victor I (AD 183-203), Gelasius (AD 492-496), and Militiades (AD 311-314). All are saints.

Source: *www.nbccongress.org*

74. (a) Ethiopia

The ancient Ethiopian monarchy maintained its freedom from colonial rule, one exception being the Italian occupation of 1936-41.

Source: Library of Congress *Country Studies*

 Who was Olaudah Equiano?

a)Explorer

b)African kidnapped from his Nigerian village at the age of eleven

c)Slaveholder

 In 1816, Captain Paul Cuffee took thirty-eight American blacks to which West African country?

a)Liberia

b)Sierra Leone

c)Ghana

ANSWERS

75. (b) African kidnapped from his Nigerian village at the age of eleven.

After ten years of enslavement, Equiano bought his freedom. At forty-four, he wrote and published his autobiography, *The Interesting Narrative of the Life of Olaudah Equiano, or Gustavus Vassa, The African.* Olaudah registered his work at Stationer's Hall, London, in 1789.

76. (b) Sierra Leone

Paul Cuffee (1759-1817), a Quaker ship owner of African and Native American ancestry, settled freed American slaves in Freetown, Sierra Leone in 1816.

Source: Library of Congress Resource Guide - *Study of Black History and Culture*

The capital of which West African country was named after the former U.S. President James Monroe?

a) Liberia

b) Sierra Leone

c) Guinea

In 1884, at the request of Portugal, German chancellor Otto von Bismarck called together the major Western powers of the world to negotiate questions and end the conflicts over the control of Africa. What was the result of the "Berlin Conference"?

a) European powers scrambled to gain control over the interior of the continent

b) Africa was divided into fifty countries

c) Ethnic groups were merged

d) all of the above

ANSWERS

77. (a) Liberia

Monrovia is the capital of Liberia. In 1817, the American Colonization Society (ACS) was formed to send free African Americans to Africa. In 1822, the society established on the west coast of Africa a colony that in 1847 became the independent nation of Liberia.

Source: Library of Congress Resource Guide - *Study of Black History and Culture*

78. (d) all of the above

de Blij, H.J. and Peter O. Muller. *Geography: Realms, Regions, and Concepts*. (New York: John Wiley & Sons, Inc., 1997)

 Who was one of was one of the founders of the NAACP (National Association for the Advancement of Colored People)?

a) W.E.B. DuBois

b) Booker T. Washington

c) Martin Luther King Jr.

 With the enactment of apartheid laws, racial discrimination was institutionalized in South Africa in which year?

a) 1863

b) 1948

c) 1998

ANSWERS

79. (a) W.E.B. DuBois

On February 12, 1909, the NAACP was founded by this multiracial group of civil rights activists: Ida Wells-Barnett; W.E.B. DuBois; Henry Moscowitz; Mary White Ovington; Oswald Garrison Villiard; William English Walling.

Source: National Association for the Advancement of Colored People

80. (b) 1948

The apartheid laws prohibited marriage between non-whites and whites, and the sanctioned "white-only'" jobs.

Source: Library of Congress *Country Studies*

 In which year did the first West African country receive its independence from colonial rule?

a) 1957

b) 1960

c) 1962

 Ghana received its independence from colonial rule in 1957. Who was leader of the Ghanaian government in 1957?

a) Haile Selassie

b) Kwame Nkrumah

c) Jerry Rawlings

ANSWERS

81. (a) 1957

Ghana was the first West African country to receive its independence from colonial rule. Ghana received its independence March 6, 1957.

Source: Nkrumah, Kwame. *Neo-colonialism: The Last Stage of Imperialism.* (New York: International Publishers, 1965)

82. (b) Kwame Nkrumah

Kwame Nkrumah (1909-1962) was Ghana's first president when it became independent in 1957

Source: Nkrumah, Kwame. *Neo-colonialism: The Last Stage of Imperialism.* (New York: International Publishers, 1965)

 On August 27, 1963, W.E.B. DuBois died in which West African country?

a) Mali

b) Ghana

c) Senegal

 *The African Origin of Civilization: Myth of Reality* was written by which Senegalese author and historian?

a) Cheikh Anta Diop

b) Joseph Ndiaye

c) Mariama Ba

ANSWERS

83. (b) Ghana

W.E.B. DuBois was born on February 23, 1868 in Great Bar-
rington, Massachusetts, and died August 27, 1963 in Accra,
Ghana.

Source: *duboislc.org*

84. (a) Cheikh Anta Diop

According to Dr. John Henrik Clarke in a 1974 paper, Cheikh
was one of the best scholars writing about Africa, and was one
of the greatest living black historians.

 Which Somalian supermodel is married to the musician/actor David Bowie?

a) Iman

b) Jan

c) Josh

 Who is a world renowned Senegalese artist from Gorée Island, Senegal?

a) Martha Dieng

b) Kambel Dieng

c) Sophie Dieng

ANSWERS

85. (a) Iman

In 1992, Iman married British musician/actor David Bow-ie.

Source: Bowie, Iman. *I Am Iman.* (New York: Universe Publishing, 2001)

86. (b) Kambel Dieng

Kambel Dieng has permanent art exhibitions in France, Holland, Africa, and the U.S.A.

Source: *au-senegal.com*

 Which Malian singer and guitarist won the 1994 Grammy Award for best world music album?

a) Ali Farka Toure

b) Meriam Makeba

c) Solle Keita

 What year marked the end of the apartheid regime in South Africa?

a) 1989

b) 1990

c) 1994

ANSWERS

87. (a) Ali Farka Toure (1939-2006)

Ali Farka Toure and Ry Cooder won the 1994 Grammy Award for best world music album for their album entitled *Talking Timbuktu.*

Source: Grammy Awards

88. (c) 1994

In February 1990, President F.W. de Klerk announced Nelson Mandela's release from prison and began the dismantling of the apartheid system. The democratic election of 1994 marked the end of the apartheid regime.

Source: Library of Congress Country Studies

 What year was Nelson Mandela elected president of South Africa?

a) 1994

b) 1995

c) 1996

 Who was elected president of South Africa in 1999?

a) Thabo Mbeki

b) P. W. Botha

c) F. W. deKlerk

ANSWERS

89. (a) 1994

Nelson Mandela was inaugurated as the State President of South Africa on May 10, 1994.

Source: Library of Congress *Country Studies*

90. (a) Thabo Mbeki

Thabo Mbeki was elected president of South Africa June 16, 1999.

Source: CIA *The World Factbook*

Chapter 8: African Quotations

This chapter supplies a quotation and you are to identify the author. Hints are supplied.

Who said, "If we have lost touch with what our fore-fathers discovered and knew, this has been due to the system of education to which we were introduced"? (Ghana's first president)

a) Kwame Nkrumah

b) Nelson Mandela

c) Haile Selassie

Who said, "The victory of democracy in South Africa is the common achievement of all humanity"? (South African statesman, 1993 Nobel Prize for Peace winner)

a) Troy Rhodes

b) Desmond Tutu

c) Nelson Mandela

ANSWERS

91. (a) Kwame Nkrumah

Source: Nkrumah, Kwame. Excerpt from speech given at the Congress of Africanists, Accra, Ghana, December 1962

92. (c) Nelson Mandela

Source: Nelson Mandela, *A Long Walk to Freedom*. (Boston: Little Brown, 1994)

 Who said, "The most potent weapon in the hands of the oppressor is the mind of the oppressed"? (Founder of the Black Consciousness movement in South Africa)

a) Steve Biko

b) Kofi Annon

c) Nelson Mandela

Who said, "…only the story can continue beyond the warrior. It is the story that outlives the sound of war-drums and the exploits of brave fighters. It is the story…that saves our property from blundering like blind beggars into the spikes of cactus fence"? (African novelist)

a) Bishop Desmond Tutu

b) Chinua Achebe

c) Nelson Mandela

ANSWERS

93. (a) Steve Biko

Source: Biko, Steve. *I Write What I Like – Selected Writings*. (Chicago: University of Chicago Press, 2002)

94. (b) Chinua Achebe

Source: Achebe, Chinua. *Anthills of the Savannah*. (New York: Doubleday, 1989)

 Who said, "From this African sanctuary of black pain, we implore forgiveness from Heaven"? (Pope visiting the slave dungeons of Gorée Island, Senegal in February 1992)

a) Pope John Paul II

b) Pope Paul

c) Pope Benedict XVI

Who said, "The toll of miseries and lives which the Negro Slave trade claimed is beyond anything one can imagine. Uprooted from their native land, driven to a foreign land, without common language, without an outright disproportion between males and females, sold out to masters at random, overburdened with hard labor and without any other education but obedience or flogging, these Blacks reduced to the status of stray individuals could not reconstitute families"? (Principal curator of the "House of Slaves" on Gorée Island, Dakar, Senegal.)

a) Bishop Desmond Tutu

b) Joseph Boubacar Ndiaye

c) Nelson Mandela

ANSWERS

95. (a) Pope John Paul II

Source: Browder, Anthony T. *Nile Valley Contributions to Civilization.* Washington, DC: The Institute of Karmic Guidance, 1992

96. (c) Joseph Boubacar Ndiaye

Source: Ndiaye, Joseph Boubacar. *The Slave House of Gorée Island.* (Senegal: 1995)

97 Who said, "When you control a man's thinking, you do not have to worry about his actions. You do not have to tell him not to stand here or go yonder. He will find his 'proper place' and will stay in it. You do not need to send him to the back door. He will go without being told. In fact, if there is no back door, he will cut one for his special benefit. His education makes it necessary"? (Father of Negro History)

a)Ivan Sentima

b)Carter G. Woodson

c)Jocelyn Mandela

98 Who said, "Once a Zambian and a South African, it is said, were talking. The Zambian boasted about their Minister of Naval Affairs. The South African asked, 'But you have no navy, no access to the sea. How then can you have a Minister of Naval Affairs?' The Zambian retorted: 'Well, in South Africa you have a Minister of Justice, don't you?'" (African spiritual leader and novelist, Nobel Prize for Peace)

a) Nelson Mandela

b) Bishop Desmond Tutu

c) Kofi Annon

ANSWERS

97. (b) Carter G. Woodson

Source: Woodson, Carter G. *The Mis-Education of the Negro.* (Washington: Associated Press, 1933)

98. (b) Bishop Desmond Tutu

Source: Tutu, Desmond. Acceptance of Nobel Peace Prize. Norwegian Nobel Institute, Oslo, Norway, 11 Dec. 1984

99 Who said, "Bringing the gifts that my ancestors gave, I am the dream and the hope of the slave. I rise I rise I rise"? (African- American poet)

a) Mari Evans

b) Maya Angelou

c) Alpha Walker

100 Who said, "The civilization of Egypt, and of Africa in general, is the most written about and the least understood of all known subjects. This is not an accident or an error in misunderstanding the available information. Except for Egypt, African people have been programmed out of the respectable commentary of history"? (African-American historian)

a) Bishop Desmond Tutu

b) Dr. John Henrik Clarke

c) Kofi Annan

ANSWERS

99. (b) Maya Angelou

Source: *And Still I Rise*, 1978

100. (b) Dr. John Henrik Clarke

Source: Browder, Anthony T. *Nile Valley Contributions to Civilization.* (Washington, DC: The Institute of Karmic Guidance, 1992)

Berlin Conference - African Scramble

MAJOR EUROPEAN COLONIAL HOLDINGS IN AFRICA AFTER THE BERLIN CONFERENCE IN 1885

Great Britain desired a Cape-to-Cairo collection of colonies, and almost succeeded through their control of Egypt, Sudan (Anglo-Egyptian Sudan), Uganda, Kenya (British East Africa), South Africa, and Zambia, Zimbabwe, and Botswana).

The British also controlled Nigeria and Ghana (Gold Coast). France took much of western Africa, from Mauritania to Chad (French West Africa), Gabon, and the Republic of Congo (French Equatorial Africa).

Belgium and King Leopold II controlled the Democratic Republic of Congo (Belgian Congo).

Portugal took Mozambique in the east and Angola in the west.

Italy's holdings were Somalia (Italian Somaliland) and a portion of Ethiopia.

Germany took Namibia (German Southwest Africa) and Tanzania (German East Africa).

Spain claimed Equatorial Guinea (Rio Muni).

Source: de Blij, H.J. and Peter O. Muller. *Geography: Realms, Regions, and Concepts.* New York: John Wiley & Sons, Inc., 1997. p. 340.

African countries and their
year of independence from colonial rule

Liberia	1847	Tanzania	1961
South Africa	1910	Sierra Leone	1961
Egypt	1922	Burundi	1962
Ethiopia	1945	Rwanda	1962
Libya	1951	Uganda	1962
Sudan	1956	Algeria	1962
Morocco	1956	Kenya	1963
Tunisia	1956	Zambia	1964
Ghana	1957	Malawi	1964
Guinea	1958	Zimbabwe	1965
Madagascar	1960	Gambia	1965
Democratic		Lesotho	1966
Republic of Congo	1960	Swaziland	1966
Gabon	1960	Botswana	1966
Somalia	1960	Equatorial Guinea	1968
Cameroon	1960	Mauritius	1968
Central African		Guinea Bissau	1974
Republic	1960	Mozambique	1975
Chad	1960	Angola	1975
Nigeria	1960	Cape Verde	1975
Benin	1960	São Tomé and	
Togo	1960	Príncipe	1975
Côte d'Ivoire		Western Sahara	1976
(Ivory Coast)	1960	Seychelles	1976
Senegal	1960	Comoros	1976
Mauritania	1960	Djibouti	1977
Niger	1960	Namibia	1990
Burkina Faso	1960	Eritrea	1993
Mali	1960		

Source: The Namibia Economist

Glossary

Akan
    A member of an ethnic group of Ghana and Côte d'Ivoire, including the Fante and the Twi.

Apartheid
    "Separateness," policy implemented by National Party government (1948-94) to maintain separate development of government-demarcated racial groups.

Asante
    Akan group, geographically located to the central part of the country. Founders of the Asante Empire, and speakers of Asante-Twi language.

Asantehene
    King of Asante.

Berbers
    A member of a North African, primarily Muslim ethnic group living from Morocco to Egypt.

diaspora
    A dispersion of a people from their original homeland.

Dogon
    People of an ethnic group who occupy a region in Mali, south of the Sahara Desert in Africa.

enclave
   A country or part of a country lying wholly within the boundaries of another.

ethnic group
   A sizable group of people sharing a common and distinctive racial, national, religious, linguistic, or cultural heritage.

griot
   An oral historian or musician in western Africa who perpetuates the oral tradition and history of a village or family.

indigenous
   Originally inhabiting an area.

Mandingo
   A Mande people of West Africa, who are descendents physically or culturally from the ancient Mali Empire.

Maasai
   A member of a chiefly pastoral ethnic group of Kenya and parts of Tanzania. Also, the language of this group.

mosque
   A Muslim house of worship.

nomad
   A member of a group that move according to seasons for food, water, and grazing land.

pharaoh
   A king of ancient Egypt.

pyramid

A massive monument of ancient Egypt having a rectangular base and four triangular faces culminating in a single apex, built over or around a crypt or tomb.

Swahili

Bantu language of the coast and islands of eastern Africa from Somalia to Mozambique. Also called Kiswahili. Also, an inhabitant of coastal eastern Africa, for whom Swahili is the mother tongue.

Tuareg

The Tuareg are known for their men's practice of veiling the face with a blue, indigo-dyed cloth. In the Sahara Desert, where most of them reside, they are known as the "Blue Men." The Tuareg men's face-veil has several different meanings.

Tutsi

Member of a minority ethnic group living in Rwanda and Burundi

UNESCO

United Nations Education Science and Cultural Organization.

Wolof

Predominant ethnic group of Senegal, living mostly in western Senegal. Also, the language of the Wolof, which has become the principal language of Senegal.

Yoruba

A member of a West African ethnic group living chiefly in southwest Nigeria.

Zulu

A member of a Bantu ethnic group of southeast Africa, primarily inhabiting northeast Natal province in South Africa.

Bibliography

au-senegal.com. 2005. Artgalerie. 2 Feb. 2006
<http:www.au-senegal.com/>.

bbc.co.uk. 2006. "The Story of Africa, An African Perspective." 20 March 2006. < http://bbc.co.uk/>.

Bowie, Iman. *I Am Iman.* New York: Universe Publishing, 2001.

Browder, Anthony T. *Nile Valley Contributions to Civilization.* Washington, DC: The Institute of Karmic Guidance, 1992.

Byrnes, Rita M., d. *South Africa: A Country Study.* Washington: GPO for the Library of Congress, 1996.

Census.gov. 2006 International Data Base.
30 May 2006 <http://www.census.gov>.

CIA.org. 2006. *The World Factbook.* 30 May 2006
<http://cia.org/>.

duboislc.org. 2006. W.E.B. DuBois. 30 Feb 2006
< http://www.duboislc.org/>.

Equiano, Olaudah. *The Interesting Narrative of the Life of Olaudah Equiano, Or Gustavus Vassa, The African.* London: Stationer's Hall, 1789.

Folkard, Claire, ed. *Guinness World Records 2004*. New York: Bantam Doubleday Dell Publishing Group, 2004.

kintehaley.org. 2006 The Kunta Kinte-Alex Haley Foundation, Inc. 5 Jan. 2006. <http://kintehaley.org/>.

maasai-association.org. Ed. Kakuta ole Maimai. 2006. Maasai Association. 24 June 2006
<http:// www.maasai-association.org >.

Mandela, Nelson. *A Long Walk to Freedom, Boston*: Little Brown, 1994.

McBrien, Richard. *Lives of the Popes: The Pontiffs from St. Peter to John Paul II*. New York: Harper Collins, 1997.

Metz, Helen Chapin, ed. *Madagascar: A Country Study*. Washington DC: GPO for the Library of Congress, 1994.

mrdowling.com. 2006. Mike Dowling. 20 June 2006. <http://www.mrdowling.com/>.

nationalgeographic.com. 2006. National Geographic. 20 Feb 2006 <http://www.nationalgeographic.com/>.

nbccongress.org. 2006. The National Black Catholic Congress, "African Popes." 4 Apr. 2006 <http:www.nbccongress. org/black-catholics/african-popes.asp/>.

Ndiaye, Joseph Boubacar. *The Slave House of Gorée Island*. Senegal: 1995.

Nkrumah, K. *Neo-colonialism: The Last Stage of Imperialism.* New York: International Publishers, 1965.

NobelPrize.org. 2006. The Nobel Foundation. 20 June 2006. <http://nobelprize.org/>.

The American Heritage° Dictionary of the English Language, Fourth Edition. Boston: Houghton Mifflin, 2000.

Tutu, Desmond. Acceptance of Nobel Peace Prize. Norwegian Nobel Institute, Oslo, Norway. 11 Dec. 1984.

Unesco.org. 2006. United Nations Education, Scientific, and Cultural Organization. 17 Jan 2006 < http://unesco.org/>.

Vanbeek, E. A., *Dogon: Africa's People of the Cliff.* New York: Harry N. Adams, 2004.

Vatican.va. 2006. "The Church and Racism: Towards a More Fraternal Society." Vatican Holy See. 20 Feb. 2006 <http://www.vatican.va/>.

Woodson, Carter G. *The Mis-Education of the Negro.* Washington: Associated Press, 1933.

Ake, Claude. *Social Science as Imperialism.* Dakar, Senegal: CODESRIA, 1982.

Asante, Molefi. *The Afrocentric Idea.* Philadelphia: Temple University Press, 1987.

Bennett Jr., A. Lerone. *Before the Mayflower.* Chicago: Johnson Publishing Co., Inc., 2000.

Davidson, Basil. *Discovering Our African Heritage.* Boston: Ginn, 1991.

Diop, Cheikh Anta. *The African Origin of Civilization: Myth or Reality.* Westport, Conn., 1974.

Karenga, Maulana. *Introduction to Black Studies.* Los Angeles, Calif.: University of Sankore, 1993.

Lumumba-Kasongo, Tukumbi. *Political Re-Mapping of Africa: Transnational Ideology and Re-definition of Africa in World Politics.* Lanham, NY, and London: University of America Press, 1994.

Wiener, Leo, with new introduction by Dr. John Henrik Clarke. *Africa and the Discovery of America.* New York: A & B Books, 1992.

Woodson, Carter G. *The Mis-Education of the Negro.* Washington: Associated Press, 1933.

www.ingramcontent.com/pod-product-compliance
Lightning Source LLC
Chambersburg PA
CBHW020255290526
45784CB00003B/1259